MW00761843

Coming & Going
... and Waiting

For Tom ~
A neighbor
and a dear
friend.

Heather
2·28·19

Coming & Going
...and Waiting

A Collection of Poems

Heather A. Gross

Writers Club Press
New York Lincoln Shanghai

Coming & Going . . . and Waiting
A Collection of Poems

All Rights Reserved © 2003 by Heather A. Gross

No part of this book may be reproduced or transmitted in any form or by
any means, graphic, electronic, or mechanical, including photocopying,
recording, taping, or by any information storage retrieval system, without
the written permission of the publisher.

Writers Club Press
an imprint of iUniverse, Inc.

For information address:
iUniverse
2021 Pine Lake Road, Suite 100
Lincoln, NE 68512
www.iuniverse.com

ISBN: 0-595-26583-9

Printed in the United States of America

In memory of our Dads . . .

William David Graham

and

Robert Lee Gross, Sr.

Contents

. . . and Waiting

In remembrance of September 11, 2001

Preface

This poetry collection, Coming & Going . . . and Waiting, has a morose subject—Death—but when you finish reading my poems, I believe you will find yourself feeling uplifted.

All of us know Death in one form or another. Just as twilight is a part of each day so is Death to a lifetime. Grief is universal. We may display our mourning in different manners but we all feel the encompassing agony and utter emptiness that calls itself Grief. We feel as if we are living in a nightmare—the experience so surreal we wonder when we will awaken and chase away this darkness. Our arms feel empty, we yearn for something to hold; we cannot sit still, yet we know not where to go. We believe if we could only sleep we would again find the one we lost. We sigh but the burden will not be lifted.

We attend the funeral desperate to share our thoughts, feelings and memories with others who validate our right to mourn. We believe that once our loved one is buried or placed in an urn, or scattered on the winds, the pain will lessen and we can go back to our lives as if nothing has changed. Yet the day after the funeral we relive it over and over again as if in savoring those moments, we can bring the lost soul home. We go to the cemetery, place flowers on the grave, speak to the soul to assuage our distress. Some of us make this pilgrimage—days marked on the calendar—an obligation to meet. As if visiting Grief on certain days keeps it from residing in your soul forever. But we cannot control Grief! As hard as we try, it will not be tamed!

Anger visits. You grab on and hope the red fury will chase away the black fear—fear of being alone. Guilt comes to call. Repeating those phrases over and over, a broken record you cannot turn off: "Why didn't I see this coming?" "Why didn't I visit sooner?" "Why didn't I say 'I love you' the last time we spoke?"

Regret will stay—setting up permanent quarters in your soul unless you let go of the twilight and say, "Good night."

Heather Gross
January 2003

For my grandmother,

Zelma Burroughs Graham,

who left her talent in my suitcase.

Coming

～ Coming & Going
... and Waiting

I.   Anticipating
Preparing
Traveling
Wondering
Coming to the day

Sunlight streaming
Under the door
Golden threads
That weave a web
Promises to behold

When will you arrive?
Entering the morning
With a smile
Full of wonder
Looking forward with hope

II. Dreading
    Wishing
    Knowing
    Giving
    Going from tomorrow

    Moonbeams dancing
    On the counterpane
    Silver strands
    That once were gold
    Speaking of the past

    Why must you go?
    Falling asleep
    With a sigh
    A full glass of water
    . . . Still

III. Expecting
      Hoping
      Watching
      Needing
      Waiting for the night

      Starlight glittering
      Silver and gold
      Today and tomorrow
      Lost in the knowledge
      Wise and weary

      Where are you now?
      A smile of sunshine
      Teardrops of rain
      Waiting . . .
      For the coming and going

🔊 *Memories of Sleep*

How does one feel
When he knows
He is dying
Fear, if he closes his
Eyes
They may never open
Again

How does life taste
Perhaps the last
Supper, food that he
Experienced
To be savored
In his thoughts
Always

How does he touch
The garments of his
Days, chores that he
Carried
As he walked
Down the road of
Yesterdays

How does he see
The people he so
Loves, everyone he
Embraced
Comes by for a visit
To say farewell
Forever

How does he hear
The sounds of his
Memories
The voices and birds
Chirping, and whispering
Winds reaching out
Tomorrow

So, how does a soul
Sleep
He closes his eyes
His life—a dream
Yesterdays live on
Until the dawn's light
Rises

∽ *Final Vision*

I saw the face
Of death today
Peering back at me
With eyes of emptiness

And just like the Reaper
The gaze of life was gone
Far away in a place
Of everlasting vision

Those final hours
Just before the journey
Saying goodbye to a soul
Who left hours ago

∾ *Going Home*

It happened during
The night
He was sleeping
His dog at his side
He dreamed of faraway
Music
A time at the Ankara

His parents were there
Spinning
On the dance floor
Elegant and remote
Smiling
But never
Laughing

The music suddenly
Stopped
His mother told him
It was time
He nodded
And set down
His clarinet

His father frowned
Peering over
His eyeglasses
And demanded to know
Where he had been
All this time
He shrugged, smiling

They toasted
"To yesterday"
The music resumed
But he didn't play
The lights dimmed
And with his parents
He waltzed from this world

Living in Shadows

When someone dies
You hear a door
Slam shut
So loud
It jars you
From this world

The Reaper appears
And reaches out
Taking
Without asking
Leaving behind
A shadow

Whether the sun
Or moon
Is shining
I only see
The darkness beyond
The candle

He died today
The door closed
Quietly—with grace
His shadow
Touched my soul
Forever

∿ *Red Skies*

Red skies
In the morning
Sailors take warning

As the sun
Opened her eyes
He closed his

For the last time
As his ship sailed
Over the horizon

He was a gentle man
He obeyed his parents
He loved his family

He honored his country
Served in the war
Sailed on the seas

He traveled the world
Yet never left home
He was the star

Bravely shining
From the paned window
Of his son's expression

He loved the sea
The wind—the sounds
Of sail and rope

The yawn of his ship
As she sailed
Through the storms

Yet he always knew
He would return
To see his family again

Now, the red skies
The star out to sea
His ship sailing . . .

Over the horizon

～ *Guiding Light*

Every weekday
At three o'clock
He watched
The *Guiding Light*

And so it was
Just before dawn
He ascended . . .
The light guiding

Him home.

ᕐ *The Leaving Room*

The leaving is much harder
Than a heavy wooden door
You may come and go
Closing past or future
Present in the room

Departing on a voyage
Without a single suitcase
Clothes left scattered
Like memories
In the corners of the room

Going down a tunnel
Where those you haven't seen
In many years
Await you with a candle
Walls weeping in the room

The leaving is a journey
That all of us will take
A last vacation
A coming and going
The room closes the door

∾ *Ordained*

I dreaded
The day
Would come
That crying
Phone call
Before the dawn

"He is gone"
And as if
I had died
My heart stopped
I couldn't breath
I couldn't see

"Where is he?"
But we didn't say
Goodbye
He must come back!
I need
One more hug

The grave was dug
In the family
Plot where they
All reside
Side by side
Dreaming of yesterday

ᔐ *Eternal Love*

How do you say goodbye
To a soul already gone
Far away in a place
Between life and death

Lying there waiting
For an angel to guide him
Up through the clouds
To the house of eternity

Wishing we could laugh
Just one last time
And talk of those memories
That only we share

So, how do you say goodbye
With a smile and a tear
Knowing that we'll meet again
In the paradise of love

❧ *Fog & Mist*

I always say
I will learn
From the past
And live
Without regrets

But I always
Forget the lessons
I continue to
Make mistakes
Etched in stone

How can I
Forgive myself
I never visited
Rarely called
And now . . . he is gone

Unspoken conversations
Whisper in my ears
Hugs never given
Yearning empty arms
Love unexpressed

I would love
To hear more of
His vast experiences
And reminisce
Such happy memories

I would love
To see his soft
Gentle smile
Feel it warm me
As winter's sun

But now
It's too late
For as the sun rose
On a hopeless morning
Fog & Mist

Enshroud me

∿ *Mort*

When Death comes to call
Do not bar the door
Invite him in
"Take tea"
Remember your life
As you chat about yesterday

Read your autobiography
Laugh and smile
"And weep"
For those you love
And will leave behind
As you walk through that door

You will not be alone
Those who have gone
"Before you"
Await your arrival
An elegant bridge party
Without cards

When Death takes you home
You need not be afraid
Close that door
"Say goodbye"
Forever knowing
We shall meet again

❧ *Land of Twilight*

I came to visit you
But found instead
A man I didn't know
A ghost awaiting death

Your eyes so glassy
Your hands so cold
Like a shrunken apple head
On a popsicle stick

You babbled away
In a language all your own
As if returning to infancy
So helpless, yet full of wonder

There were so many things
That I wanted to say
But the sun had set
Gone to bed for the day

And so like a mother
With a babe in her arms
I crooned you to sleep
To the land of twilight

❧ *The War*

Your room is filled
With medical equipment
A hospital bed
A nutrition pump
An IV pole
An air mattress
A wheelchair
Sitting in silence
When will you return?

You fought valiantly!
With your room left in limbo
You lay in the hospital
A machine—your lungs
A monitor—counting time
In heartbeats
With battalions of nurses marching
And doctors—
The cavalry

I watched your battle
Knowing you grew tired
How I just wanted
To pick up your gun
And fight in this war!
My strength could be yours
And in the quiet lull
That follows the carnage
I would carry you home

Now I wait
To honor the dead
With a lone trumpet
Playing *Taps*
In the echoes
I see you
Closing your eyes
One last time
Never to return

∾ *The Obituary*

The death notice
Was so empty
The name—the family
The town—the place
Of death
So hollow

A life was lived
And then disappeared
As if a fog
Stole those moments
Leaving behind
Just black and white

What were his dreams
Those hopes and wishes
Realized or vanished
Did he laugh
At the moon
Or dance in the rain

So many stories
Words never written
Lives that had meaning
Never to be
Revealed
Hidden behind life's veil

∾ *Gertrude*

As the sun
Rose on a red
Sky an evening
Star hung on
The horizon
Waiting . . .

For his coming
Her son was
Born on the day
She cast out
To sea
A ship

Reaching for
Her port—his
Boundless love
Anchoring her
A safe harbor
Beckoning

But the red
Tide was not
High enough
To pull her
From the rocky
Coast

Embracing waves
Capturing her
Between land &
Sea and Gertrude
Is sinking . . .
Going

As her son
Smiled for the
First time
The sun set
As she
Whispered

"There is no sadness in farewell."

﹏ *"I'm sorry."*

"I'm sorry."
His last words
To me
And then he died
Before I could ask
What he meant

Was he sorry
For the war . . .
Leaving me behind
After his wife died
To run from grief
And his motherless child?

Was he sorry
For never talking
About his feelings?
For never sharing
His greatest loss
With the son who missed her, too?

Was he sorry
For not bonding
With his firstborn?
For each time
He saw me
He remembered her, too.

Was he sorry
For not calling
More often?
For not visiting?
For not suggesting
We get away together . . .

Just father and son?
Now, I sit here
Your words haunting
Me . . . I wish
I had said
"I'm sorry, too."

❧ Sunday

She died this morning
As the last dew
Dropped from the tree
Sleeping peacefully
In the sunlight
She vanishes . . .

I see her
Lily in the Valley
Purest white blossoms
Small but very strong
A soul so filled
With love

The little birds
Who grace her yard
Will always remember
Her loving ways
They sing the saddest
Songs of sorrow

She died today
As twilight nears
We reach out
Embrace the night
In the brightest star
. . . She reappears

~ *Holding Hands*

When I came
To see you
At the hospital
It had been awhile
Since our last
Visit

The doctor said
There wasn't
Much time
So I drove
Through the night
Fear in my heart

I arrived before
Dawn—lost
In the dark
I crept into
Your room
Wondering . . . hoping

You opened your eyes
A smile beckoned
You held out
Your hand
I took it
In mine

How strong
Your grip was!
Neither
Of us wanted
To let go
"How did you know . . .

Where to find me?"
He asked
"I followed the stars."
I told him
He chuckled
His eyes twinkling

So many words
Were spoken
That only our souls
Could hear
"I love you."
"I love you, too."

"Don't leave."
"I will always
Be with you."
And holding hands
We sat in silence
. . . Conversing

❧ January

He went home today
I know
Because the sun
Shines brightly
His brilliant smile
Melting the snow

When he died
It was raining
I wept
And as the sun set
On his days
It was this I must accept

For the last time
I put away his laundry
His room
A tomb of memories
Voices in the echoes
Lost in yesterday

I stopped in the doorway
Trapped between today
And tomorrow
It's so hard to let go
When you know
This is goodbye

With Spring
My pain will thaw
Puddles of tears
That once were snow
And flowers waiting
For his brilliant smile

∾ *Interment*

A gathering
Birds in a field
Breaking bread
Speaking of loved ones
Who migrated
Just one last time

A ceremony
Perched on a hill
Growing with stone
Speaking of loved ones
Who disappeared
Like mist into twilight

A reunion
Those you cannot see
Giving us comfort
Speaking of loved ones
Who live
Beyond life—eternity

A parting
A delicate flower
Learning to grow
Speaking with eloquence
That secret
Of the ages

✒ *The Visitation*

As I gazed at her
I expected
Her eyes to open
Twinkling
With mischief

But she continued
To dream
A soft smile
Teasing
Her lips

Her delicate hands
Slept serenely
Flowers graced
The cloud
Of blankets

Visitors stood
Silently remembering
Moments shared
Retrieved
. . . Relived

Tears became
Words
Souls conversing
Speaking beyond
Forever

When I said goodbye
I knew
She heard me
I felt her love
Embrace me

❧ *Such Morbid Questions!*

When you die
do you cease
to feel
pain?

Do you hover
above
watching . . .
and waiting?

Do you read
your obituary?
do you smell
your bereavement flowers?

In the evening
after visitation
does the funeral parlor
close your coffin?

Why do I feel
so strange about
leaving you
at the funeral home

to return
tomorrow
to visit
your body?

❧ *For the Birds*

Driving to the cemetery
I thought
You would be there
Welcoming friends
Sharing memories
Saying a prayer
"Hello"

When I was a child
You were my favorite
Playmate
You made housework fun
Cooking an adventure
And TV golf
Interesting

Every morning
You walked the dog
And if a bird
Bid you a good morning
You would look up
And whistle
"Hello"

The funeral
Took place in February
Icy patches of dirty snow
Mourners
Crying silent tears
And a lone bird wailing
"Goodbye"

❧ *Fiction*

The funeral is over
And now I sit here
In this somber room
Waiting ...

I stand and I pace
Look out the window
Wonder what it is
That I wait for

Do I wait for you
To return and say
"It wasn't real
I never died"

∿ *Novel*

It all started
When you fell
The beginning of
Those final chapters
In a book
You cannot put down

A family drama
A story of life
Dreading the day
We reach the last
Page . . . final sentence
Last word

Period.

∽ *Still Life*

The flowers sit
In utter silence
The funeral over
The mourners are gone
And I am alone
Surrounded by your
Comforting balm

The night we danced
Our anniversary
Truly believing
We would always be
Together—forever
My heart filled
With your perfume

I touch a rose
Inhale your aroma
That summer day
Lost in our garden
Our eyes mesmerized
As we embraced
Each other's scent

Twilight has fallen
The flowers are fading
Soft petals perish
Despite fervent efforts
To keep you alive
Redolence
. . . Still life

⮌ *The Widow*

She is ever beautiful
In her grief
Eyes sparkling like jewels
Glisten on the sea

Her sobs are silent
The kind you can feel
Shadows like nightmares
Crawl in the echoes

Her shoulders are strong
Bearing this misery
Storm clouds like shrouds
Steal all the laughter

She is ever frail
In her mourning
Eerie howls like the wolf
Alone in the dark

❧ *Reflections*

I never lost
A soul
Who lived in my house
And now it feels
So empty—so restless
So alone

Acute grief
Knocking at my door
Stealing my days
Haunting my dreams
Voices of yesterday
Heard in every room

I turn on the light
To chase away the darkness
But it only
Illuminates
The startling fact
That he is forever gone

I pace the hallways
My arms—so empty
What have I forgotten
To do
I gaze out the window
Seeing only my reflection

I know he is now
With those he loved
And lost
And so I will wait
To see him again
. . . The house sighs

ᦡ *Just Waiting*

It's been a week
That you've been gone
Shoes still waiting
Under a coffee table
A coat hanging around
By the door

Your glasses view the world
Without your perspective
Your bed wonders
Where you've gone
The house holds it's breath
Just waiting

And still . . .
You haven't returned
Yet in some ways
You've never gone
For I see you there
In every room

. . . and Waiting

Most Loyal Friend

He is waiting
By the door
As if a parent
Keeping vigil
Until his life returns

He is pacing
In the yard
Tending the garden
Watching every car
Go by—never stopping

He is sleeping
With one eye open
Watching sunlight
Move into shadows
But time stands still

He is wandering
Aimless and empty
The house sighs
His footsteps lonely
The door remains closed

He is waiting
Yet he knows
His master
Will not be back
He cries without tears

∽ *Desolation*

You cannot run from Grief
A highwayman lurking
In the shadows
He may come upon you
On this road of life
At any moment

You cannot hide from Sorrow
A poacher hunting
In the forest
Aiming his arrow of misery
At your broken heart
On every hour

You cannot fight off Woe
A dangerous pirate
Stalking your days
Boarding your ship
Commanding your life
On any given day

You cannot escape Sadness
A pilferer stealing
Months of your life
Swindling your soul
Of much needed rain
During the growing season

You cannot elude the Mourning
Just as the sun
Breaks the horizon
Anguish will come
To share your Despair
And you will invite him in

❧ *He Lingers . . .*

I can still hear
His voice
The deep, rich baritone
Soothing—as he expressed
His thoughts

I can still embrace
His words
The intonation pronounced
Captivating—as he disclosed
His reveries

I can still remember
Our conversations
An abstract feast
Delicious—as he challenged
My beliefs

I can still
Touch his dreams
I close my eyes—listening
As his utterance
Lingers . . .

❧ The Dream

I saw you last night
So filled with vitality
Eyes twinkling
Smile beckoning
You were so alive!

I touched you last night
An enchanting dance
Hands touching
Hearts beating
We were so alive!

I spoke to you last night
A tender conversation
Voices mingling
Souls embracing
The phone . . . suddenly went dead

I awakened
The phone in my hand
Did you call from beyond
And kiss me in the night?
You were so alive!

Immortally Yours

Grief has become
My most intimate stranger
Lying next to me
In bed at night
Whispering
In my ear

I embrace Grief
For it knows my heart
So alone
Heavy with regret
"I need to see you
One last time"

I reside with Grief
Everyday is a storm
Hearing your voice
In the other room
"I need to talk to you
One last time"

Grief will always be
My most intimate friend
In bed with me
Holding me close
Letting me love you
Till the end of time

∾ *The Highlands*

His soul
Was born
In the Highlands
Centuries ago
Ancestors
Proud and strong

His mother
A Scottish
Lass born
In the heather
Reared in
The church

One did not
Work on Sunday
No football
Never swearing
Her cottage
Always clean

She taught
Her boys
Poetry
Gave them
Words
That always . . .

Brought them
Comfort
When her
Sons died
There was
Poetry

Found
Among their things
As if an
Echo
Still alive
In the Highlands

∾ *The Golf*

I'm missing you today
Even more
Than I usually do
I look through old
Albums filled
With memories
Days when we smiled

I talk to you
Sometimes
As if you were
Here
With me
Making dinner
While watching the golf

I miss you most
At night
I hear your saxophone
Wailing the blues
But then I wake up
And you
Are not here

I'm mourning you
Tomorrow
Yesterday and today
Every moment
You are here
In my heart
In my dreams

❧ Chess

I dreamed of him
Last night
The room was alive
With family and friends
But we were alone
Just me and Dad

We played chess
His moves sure
Me—hanging back
Not clear which pieces
Would move on
To fight the battle

He smiled patiently
It will take time
To master the game
Some pieces are taken
Struck down in the battle
But you hold on and fight

Our game was interrupted
His king fell
Never to stand again
I put the board away
Knowing that the game
Would continue on

. . . Forever

ᓚ *Grim Reaper*

When someone you love
dies
You die too
In that crystal clear
moment
Your heart ceases
to beat

No one can explain
death
You have to meet him
yourself
And once you have
your life is
Forever changed

How could you understand
such finality
Words do not
express
The total desolation
the disquietude
in your heart

Now, you've met the
Reaper
Your soul embraced
the night
You sigh
You breath
You live

❦ *The Wave*

The last time
I saw you—you
Were sitting in bed
We shared
A fragmented
Conversation
Interruptions
And mortality

How would I know
You—you looked
So different
Somehow
Yet the warmth
In your eyes
Unmistakable
You

Those moments
Seemed to drag
At the time
For you—you
Suffered
Yet never
Told
A soul

How I wish
I could have
Helped you—you
Who helped
Everyone
No matter the
Cost to
Yourself

I remember
The last time
I saw you—
You waved
As I stood
In the hall
Just beyond
Eternity

﹏ *Somewhere in Yesterday*

Oh, how we remember
The smallest of moments
As if it were
Just yesterday

In the darkness
I'd lie awake
Waiting for the Sandman
Who was always late

I'd call out
And you would come
Tell me a story
Or just reassure me

One time
You told me
Just close your eyes
And be somewhere beautiful

I obeyed
I closed my eyes
Listening to your footsteps
Mark time

Now, sitting here
Closing my eyes
I see you
Somewhere beautiful

❧ *Winter Shadows*

What happens to the
Daughter
When her Father
Passes on
No matter her age
The Daughter remains
Daddy's little girl

An echo in her heart
A hole in her soul
He was always there
To listen, love
And share
Her thoughts and her feelings
Her life

But now he is gone
And she struggles
To find herself
She could look
In his eyes
And see her
Reflection . . .

Winter has come
A mirror of ice
Frozen in time
She stands in the
Shadows—waiting
For her Father
To carry her home

❧ *Echoes*

Mother is never home
Now that Dad
Is gone
That silent void
Echoes
In every room
Haunting her days
And dreams

She attends church
Plays cards
With other widows
And once a week
She is out
To lunch
Pretending that all
Is the same

But the grief is there
In photographs
And books
That must go back
To the library
Stories told
But never heard
Lost in the echoes

❧ Never to Return

A moment lost
Forever cries on the wind
A mournful wail
A ship lost at sea
Never to return
A sunken treasure

A moment remembered
Forever shines like the moon
A spotlight
Shimmering shadows made clear
A candle flame
A smile in the dark

A moment forgotten
Forever thunders on the tide
Footsteps stolen
Once marked in the sand
Never to return
As one

A moment shared
Forever dances like the stars
Twinkling gems
Those precious secrets
A shining memory
A heavenly portrait

A moment lost
Forever echoes in the rain
A clock in time
Tears of regret
Never to return
To give back the day

◆ Bereavement

Grief has become
A telemarketer
Calling at all hours
To take away
The momentum of life
Time stands still
While I visit the "passed"

"Mourning"
Comes with the dawn
Ever so empty
I wander the house
Hold your possessions
Close to my heart
Willing you to return

I miss you today
Even more than yesterday
Gazing at your photographs
I can almost pretend
You're in the next room
Your heartbeat
Keeping time with the rain

Raindrops splatter
On the window "pain"
Tears forever present
In my "daze"
Come back—if just for a moment
Let me tell you
I love you . . .
            Just one last time

ᕦ Secret & Songs

I used to fear the tears
But now they are welcome
A gentle Spring rain
Or raging Autumn storm

The sobs are the thunder
Crashing open doors
Revealing dark rooms
That I left behind

Those times it seems calm
A lightning does strike
Fireflies in the night
Telling secrets—singing songs

So, where is the storm
For this calm rages on
Flashing sparks of Summer
And Winter knows too much

The Blanket

It is snowing
And unless you are looking
You would never know it
So silently powerful
This blanket embracing

It was snowing
The last time you called
Excited by the storm
Like a child
Who dreams of a sleigh ride

Snowflakes decorate
Windows and trees
People hibernate
Like sleepy bears
Under this winter blanket

The wind howls
As if spirits speak
And we listen
... And embrace
In this twilight

The snow is falling
And you are gone
A cold emptiness prevails
That even this blanket
Cannot melt

∾ *The Wolf*

I wait and I wait
For this weight
To be lifted
From the heart of my soul

For I know that I must
Meet my grief
Invite him to enter
Allow him to speak

Yet I fear this dreaded
Visit, never knowing
When he will leave
And if he will steal my soul

And if we do not talk
How will I continue
To live in this forest
Empty echoes—dark and cold

So, come to me grief
And allow me to mourn
To wail loudly and passionately
A lone wolf in the night

∾ *Not Now!*

Here it comes
Again
And so
I sigh
Please let
This pain
Go away!

Tears tease
My vision
I swallow
Hard
Passed
The lump
In my throat

I yearn
For his
Hug
I ache
Everywhere
Straining
To hear

His voice
I stand
Walk around
Aimlessly
I feel like
I should
Do something

But what?!
I cannot
Think
I feel
Lost
Yet I can't
Find . . .

A way out
Of this
Nightmare
I feel
Like everyone
Can tell
I'm different

As if my
Grief
Is a neon
Sign
"Here is
The walking
Dead"

Some days
I cry
Other days
I'm numb
Or confused
Or reminiscing
All day long

The tears
Are coming
Again
Not now!
I need to
Go to work
And pretend

I'm just fine

❧ *The Locket*

The locket
With your photograph
Listens to my heartbeat
As we walk through the daze

In this darkness
That is the day
I take warm comfort
That we are together

Even though I will never
See you again
For you went beyond
Tomorrow

❧ *Facade*

What a dreary day
This has become
I woke up pretending
That nothing had changed
The sun was shining
So warm for January
. . . Facade

And now it rains
A steady stream
Of tears
Falling from the heavens
He is happy to be home
Yet he longs
For all that was familiar

Oatmeal & banana
A cup of coffee
Images to start his day
So very tired
At eighty-seven
Yet he never
Stayed in bed

Saturdays brought
Football games
And on special days
The horses ran
He spoke of yesterday
Riding through fields
Defying time

Sailing a ship
Rounding the "Horn"
He was a willing vagabond
Who after many years
Reached out
And embraced love
Then returned

As I watch a cat
Drift through the rain
And shake herself dry
As she stands on her porch
I see him—a stallion
Crossing the finish line
... Alone

⮜ Disquietude

I feel lost today
I know not why
I hear that weeping child
Inside my soul
But I cannot console her

I am invisible today
A ghost in shoes
Walking through my weary chores
Yet I am not there
Alone with my reflections

I am forsaken today
A battlefield—now quiet
Alone with the carnage
I must move on
Yet I embrace this despair

I will return tomorrow
The war shall end
I shall bury my desolation
Next to my grief
And find myself again

∾ *Your Whisper is the Wind*

I have often
Found myself
Sitting there
In front of
That hospital
As if it were
The night
You died

It was winter
Yet the trees
Held on
To garment leaves
That crumbled
At a touch
Your whisper
Is the wind

Before dawn
A warm glow
Escapes from
A window
Houses stand
Sentinel
Shadows in
A graveyard

A door
Opens a man
Walks a dog
Other lights
Appear in
Happy houses
The street
Has awakened

Yet I am
Alone . . . sitting
In the darkness
The night
Unwilling to
Release the
Lonely street
In my memory

⮦ *So Many . . .*

She left this world
Very rich
Friends—relatives
So many
Who loved her

Years of photographs
Snapshots of life
Every day—holidays
So many
Moments shared

She always gave
A smile
Hugs—kisses
So many
Expressions of love

She knew how
To listen
Wisdom—compassion
So many
Helpful suggestions

She left this world
A richer place
The lives of all
Those she loved
Forever touched . . .

By her grace

ᴗ *The Other Side of the Moon*

I cannot write
A poem for you
Now that you have gone afar
Because you are
My inspiration

I miss you
Each day more than the last
What is it like
On the other side
Of the moon?

When you died
I heard my heart break
I felt you
Pass through
My soul

Leaving pawprints
Forever—on my heart
And when I smile
I feel you
With me

You wrote this poem
Not I
For my heart speaks
In your voice
. . . Always

～ *All I want for Christmas*

For Christmas this year
I got a sense
Of foreboding
Reminding me
Of an earlier Christmas
When our Uncle died

The Christmas tree
Seemed so loud
And garish
Buying gifts
Brought no joy
Nothing seemed to matter

He was in the hospital
And then the home
It seemed he would
Recover
But then the phone
Rang in the night

"He is taking a turn
For the worse."
And before we could
Come . . . he had Gone
A Christmas light
Extinguished

All I wanted
For Christmas
Was just a few
More moments
With my Dad
A gift that would

Have lived . . . forever

❧ *The Sweater*

Oh, how I regret
We said no goodbye
I had no idea
The Grim Reaper was near
To teach you how to die

A lump in my throat
A pain in my heart
I had no idea
The one I hold dear
Was about to depart

My arms are so empty
I've nothing to hold
I reached for your sweater
It made me feel better
Much richer than gold

So, when I want a hug
I find I have you
There in the wool
It's colors so full
My regrets, barely a few

A Whisper

A holiday without you is:
A cracked Easter egg;
An overcooked Thanksgiving turkey;
An undecorated Christmas tree;
Valentine's Day with a broken heart.

What is:
Thunder without lightning?
A bed without two pillows?
A rose without thorns?
Each day without a hug?

Imagine:
Wine without cheese;
Halloween without candy;
A Martini without an olive;
Ice cream melted—a puddle.

Music sounded happier when you were here
Phones rang more often
We went out to dinner
Entered magazine contests
Living with hope . . .

Remember:
Autumn's brilliant colors?
Winter's lacey snowfall?
Spring's fragrant bouquet?
Summer's warm embrace?

It is snowing now
Angelic flakes drifting
So silently on the breeze
As if you heard my thoughts
And whispered

∿ *The Tree*

The day after you died
I stood gazing
Out the front window
Remembering a tree
Who once stood proud
Providing shade
On hot summer days

And you were the tree
Each branch a year
Of your life
A base branch
The war
Each twig—a friend
A memory

My eyes climbed higher
The branches of our lives
The final years
Our many holidays
Sitting on the porch
The first days of summer
Sunlight on the leaves

One day you watched
As the utility company
Hacked off branches
Years that were gone
But never forgotten
Lying on the path
Of life

The tree died that winter
Too many branches lay
Spent on the roadside
But I still see that
Tree
Standing proud
Forever summer

❧ *Hope*

I am blind
With grief
I cannot see
Beyond this moment
Every minute an hour
Every hour a day

Groping in darkness
Reaching
Wishing
Crying out for yesterday
The nights are long
Dreams haunted by clouds

Do you watch me
Tossing with pain
And fear
Life without you
Is so empty
A house without furniture

Time crawls by
The rain comes less
Often
I see the laughter
And hear the smile
My dreams are filled with hope

∿ *I'll Never Forget*

I'll never forget . . .
How playful you were
As if a child
You played with your girls
On outdoor excursions
On game boards indoors

I envied your girls
My parents didn't play
With the same abandon
For you could get lost
In the laughter
Of a child's fantasy

The girls would get tired
But you never flagged
Your eyes all aglow
Your heart filled with pride
Two daughters you raised
Your soul full of love

And now . . . you are gone
Vanished in the fog
As if in a fairytale
Your laugh lingers
On the breeze
. . . I'll never forget

Going.

❧ *And You Must Endure*

What is it like
To be the last standing
Your comrades are gone
Lying dead at your feet
Yet the battle rages on
And you must
Survive

How do you feel
To be the last flower
Alone in the garden
The others have perished
And wilt in the weeds
And you must
Abide

How do you know
You are the last raindrop
To fall from the sky
A ripple in the water
The water of the sea
And you must
Subsist

What is it like
To be the last sibling
Your family of childhood
Gone from this world
Their voices—the wind
And you must
Live on

∾ *Encore*

Missing you
Is a forever thing
Time goes by
And I remain broken
A puddle of tears
Fill the hole in my soul

I have no umbrella
No shelter
From this storm
Thundering sobs
Flashes of anger
Torrents of misery

Then suddenly
The winds calm
The clouds open
Curtains on a stage
The sun returns
For an encore

∾ *Battlefields*

I'll never forget
That summer visit
The brothers
Sitting on the porch
Sharing their past
Happy memories
And of course
. . . The War

Their voices hushed
As they traveled
In time
Glenn Miller
Smoky canteens
The salty smell
And gentle roll
Of the sea

I peeked out
The screen door
To offer them
Refreshments
And I saw
Two young men
Not eighty something
Gentlemen

I quickly disappeared
Listening as I walked
Gentle voices
Resuming their
Cadence—marching
Off to war
To buddies
Long remembered

There is an
Unspoken code
Among soldiers
You fight
To return home
But you never
Leave
The Battlefield

The brothers
Are both gone
Now ... together
On the battlefield
Reunited
With their comrades
Who never
Came home

~ *Visits*

My grief visits
Once a week
Like a dental appointment
I dread
But must endure

During your illness
Time stood still
Each day
You withered away
And I held my breath

I visited often
Needing to see you
The way that you were
Wondering each time
"Is this our goodbye?"

Now, you are gone
And strangely
I feel relieved
Tomorrow comes
. . . I exhale

∿ *Breathless*

The other day
I was in
The grocery store
I saw this frail
Old man
Trying to select
His weekly meals
Careful—his money
Was sparse

Breath was knocked
Out of me
I suddenly saw
My Dad
Standing there
So alone and forlorn
Struggling to
Survive—his cap
Was crooked

I fought the
Urge to run
To his side
To embrace him
Give him money
Let him know
He was not
Alone—his glasses
Were dusty

I sighed . . .
And swallowing hard
I ingested
My grief
All these years
Later
I was shopping
Backwards—reaching out
To the passed

❧ Grief Resigned

This is the winter
Of our discontent
Trees that are sleeping
Appear to be dead
Silent statues of grace

The snow that fell
Is melting now
Dirty and hollow
Without the pure soul
Calm blankets with holes

The air is serene
And thoughtful now
Light and fragrant
With unborn flowers
Quiet messages of love

This is the winter
Of our moving on
The heavens are smiling
For he has come home
A stillness—a peace

❧ *My Favorite Valentine*

It's raining again
A very gloomy day
A day to reflect
To hear a saxophone wail
In my distant thoughts
And wish you were still here

It's Valentine's Day
A very somber day
A day to remember
To go to the cemetery
Place a rose on your grave
Speak to you as if you were here

Every Valentine's Day
Is a day to remember
Peering through your dusty glasses
A smile in your voice
Reaching out—embracing you
And suddenly, you are here

It's snowing now
A day of discontent
Knowing you are here
But unable to touch you
Forever my valentine
Always in my heart

❧ *St. Andrew*

You were with him
When he died
As he lay there
In his darkened bedroom
You stood by his side
Your compassionate gaze
Telling him
It was okay to go home

You promised him
You would watch over her
Protect her—keep her company
Share her grief
Make the house feel
Less empty
Be the sunrise
On the longest nights

And now . . .
You are gone
On Valentine's Day
You heard his voice
Calling your name
Leading you home
You fulfilled your promise
The sun set

I see you so clearly
Wagging your tail
Walking so proudly
Next to his footsteps
And on the long nights ahead
She'll go out in your yard
Gaze towards the heavens
And smile

～ *The Cemetery*

The cemetery
Is a timeless place
No matter the time
The day
The season
You are in the past

A serene place
Whispers on the wind
Reliving moments
If only
We could
Turn back time

Comforting—yet agonizing
A touch you cannot feel
You trace the words
Upon the stone
Leaving flowers
To die tomorrow

The cemetery
The past—the present
Whispering "I love you"
Words in the wind
That echo forever
In your soul

❧ *The Haunting*

"Do you believe
In ghosts
For when I die
I shall return
To haunt your days
Thereafter"

I wanted to
Believe—yet
I feared disappointment
I hoped he would
Return and make
Me laugh again

I knew there was
An afterlife
The soul to live
Beyond the rainbow
But could that spirit
Reach out to me

"I now believe
In eternity
For when I die
I shall reunite
With all those ghosts
Everafter"

～ *Bewitched*

I wish I had a photograph
Of you . . . playing your saxophone
Filling the kitchen
With delicious sounds
Cooking jazz

Even outside I could hear
You playing . . . big band tunes
Turning back the clock
With "Stardust Memories"
Smokin' Miller

Inside the house the melody
Was alive . . . ghosts lost in time
Haunting my days
With seductive "Bewitched"
Filling my soul

I have a photograph
Of you . . . playing your saxophone
Alone in the kitchen
As if you never left
This world

❧ *Onion Tears*

The other evening
I was in the kitchen
Making dinner
While listening to music
Suddenly a song
Seized my heart

"You are there"
It's been years since
You died
But sometimes
It feels
Like yesterday

In the summer
I hear you outside
Cutting the grass
And then we would
Sit on the porch
Sipping lemonade

As twilight falls
I watch for the
Fireflies—twinkling stars
I catch one
And show you
Then, we watch it fly away

How you loved
To read
On that porch
We shared
Such a
Comfortable silence

As the song ended
I felt tears on my cheeks
My husband noticed
He asked what was wrong
"They're onion tears"
I lied . . . smiling

We shared dinner
That evening
In a comfortable silence

❧ *Shalome*

Sitting with your ailing
Friend
Through the darkest hours
Of the longest night
Waiting . . .

She came to you
When just a kitten
Looking for comfort
And love
Coming . . .

So many times
She sat on your lap
Enjoying your warmth
As you enjoyed
Her inner strength

Over the years
She went from kitten
To little girl
To best friend
And back again

For on this night
She was your kitten again
Helpless and tired
Taking a cat nap
Going . . ..

✑ Springtime

She is the lilacs
So lovely in Springtime
Delicately fragrant
Drifting
On the breeze
So pure
So alive . . .

When my Dad died
I turned to gardening
And she was there . . .
We talked flowers
And gardens
Somehow she knew
I needed her

Her very presence
Calmed me
Filled me with hope
Made me realize
It wasn't the flowers
I needed . . . to live
Again

Grief kills you
Inside . . . a dark
Void filled with echoes
Seeking the sun
And flowers
To be born . . .
And loved

She was the lilacs
Alive in the Springtime
Now, every year
When her bush
Is in bloom
She drifts on the breeze
... Forever

∿ *Mother & Daughter*

They were friends
Matching salt
And pepper shakers
Sitting on a shelf
For fifty years

When Mother was younger
They traveled together
Went shopping
Had lunch
Moments are memories

In the summer
They would sit
On the porch
Talk about yesterdays
Dream about tomorrows

When Daughter was a child
She was nurtured
Encouraged, loved
Given strength
To endure life's travails

Time goes by
Quickly—the years
Become days
The Daughter is Mother
A candle in the dark

Salt and pepper shakers
Sitting on a shelf
Dreams of yesterday
Memory moments
Living on forever

❧ Mother's Gift

You knew before
I even sensed it
A soul began
Beyond the clouds
So nurtured
In your loving hands

When I learned
I was pregnant
I wished
You were still here
How proud you would be
How excited!

So many mother
Daughter chats
We would never share
My questions
Your wisdom
. . . and shopping!

I began to mourn
The times we would
Never have
Sometimes I smiled
When inside
I was crying

One night I dreamed
You sat in a rocking chair
There—in my room
Smiling with pride
You opened your arms
Giving me life

Days after your
Visit
I learned I was
With child
And now in my
Musing I remember

Your gift

∾ *Dad*

He was always
Optimistic
Nothing was
Impossible
Even when all
Seemed lost
He found it

The War
Was hell
During a battle
A comrade
Fell overboard
With one arm
He saved his life

A house fire
He went outside
Firemen told him
No—but he
Climbed up
A drain spout
Saving a woman's life

No matter
Life's travails
He wore a smile
He found a way
To see it through
With blood
Or sweat or tears

He will always
Be our hero
Strong and brave
The calm in a
Storm
Protector . . . now
Guardian angel

∿ 88

They were
Eighty-eight
When they died
Brothers who
Loved life
And each other

One special
Holiday they
Visited their
Childhood
Neighborhood
And home

The little house
On Page Street
During the
Depression that
House was a
Castle

A mother
And dad
Who raised
Strong brave
Men—war
Heroes

Their ships
Passed in the
Starlit sea
Yet they knew
Their brother
Was near

Years went by
Sometimes they
Dreamed
They were back
Out to sea
Lost . . . afraid

Then suddenly
You became
Him—his
Beloved brother
There
To save him

"How did you
find me?"
They both
Would ask
A warm smile
A sudden knowledge

No matter where
They were
They knew
They would
Be together
In this world

. . . and beyond

❧ *Heaven Can't Wait*

He loved baseball
When they were young
He let them go
With him to see
The minor league
Play their games

One son changed
The scoreboard
While the younger
Took the tickets
And after the game
They went to a pub

While grandpap helped
To count the earnings
The brothers
Swept the floor
They earned sandwiches
How good they tasted!

Those days were
Special—memories
That guided them
As they grew up
Worked hard . . . keeping
Those family traditions

Now, there is a
Baseball game
Far beyond the clouds
A father proud
Of two fine sons
Crossing home plate at last

⤳ *Inspirit*

She was the epitome
Of beauty
Grace and style
All who knew her
Were inspired

She was the essence
Of kindness
Caring and patience
All who loved her
Were cherished

She was the sun
Warm and welcoming
Embracing you
In her gentle
Radiance

She was a star
So bright and delicate
Captivating you
With her expressive
Talent

She is forever alive
In memories
Her quiet manner
Touching our hearts
With everlasting joy

❧ Calendar Lost in Time

I went into your room
Today
And tried to clear the past
Away
Pack up clothes, and shoes, and books
Take down pictures that lived on hooks

But I could not follow
Through
The room was yearning to see only
You
As if you were alive and well
Throw away my grief and perpetual hell

Eyeglasses that will never see
Sleeping books & comatose pens
Handicapped shoes and
Languishing canes
Bereaved blankets
A calendar lost in time . . ..

Will I ever let you go?
Will your room become a shrine?
Will the grief quit choking me?
Will a holiday ever be happy?
Will your ghost stop haunting me?
No, for you shall forever reside

In my heart

∾ *The Mourning Rain*

Grief came back for a visit
An unwelcome "morning"
It's been nearly a year
Since you departed
Yet it feels like yesterday

I resist the tears
Who threaten to "reign"
Should I open the door
I blink in fury
And summon my anger

I'm in pain again
And I don't want to hurt!
A dark abyss
I am lost
With nowhere to run

Such a lump in my throat
An intruder pushing against
The door of my soul
I bolt the door
Yet it's only a matter of time

My arms are so empty
Longing to hold you
I gaze at your photograph
Tears teasing my vision
I open an umbrella

. . . and sigh

∿ *The Darkened Room*

It's been a year
It's time to let go
To allow your ghost
To leave my house
And dance under the stars

Dust motes linger
On the silent TV
The phone wonders
When it will ring
The light bulbs never smile

Your desk ponders
Where you have gone
Your shoes know
They will never again
Run in the rain

The rocking chair sits
Unmoving—depressed
The window blinds
Wink at the tree
So lonely in the moonlight

Your pictures hang around
Suspended in time
Your comforter waits
To embrace a new owner
The darkened room . . .

Now filled with sunlight

The Watch

Time stopped
I knew the very moment
You left this world
I felt a black void
Fill the space around me
A room without a light

Time dragged on
Every moment of the day
Lasted forever
I couldn't believe
You would never again
Light my house with your smile

Time stood still
As I relived each moment
We ever shared
Pretending you were still here
Living alongside me
The sun on the porch

Time stopped
Suddenly I realized
That you were really gone
We settled your affairs
I began feeling your presence
As I wore your beloved watch

Time stopped
A year to the day
To the minute
To the exact second
You said to me
"I love you, too."

For the last time

∾ *Today & Tomorrow*

Why is it
All these years later
It feels as if you
Just died
Today

That yearly
Anniversary brings
The rain—tears
From the clouds
Above

I am feeling
So empty—a mausoleum
Haunted by
Memories ever
Alive

I cry out
Your name—as if
I expect you
To answer
Forever

You are gone
I am lost
Yet I know—I
Will see you
Tomorrow

～ *Death is Survival*

Death
Is change
Overcoming fear
Of a different existence
The being
You loved
Is no longer
Here
And yet
You're not alone

Death
Is survival
Embracing tomorrow
Learning how to cope
Adjusting
To pain
Strengthening
Your resolve
Standing strong
On your own

Death
Is knowledge
Remembering yesterday
Coping with regrets
Understanding
Forgiving yourself
Being thankful
For life's lessons
The seasons of change
To grow . . . or pass on

⁓ Seasons Recall

Did you ever notice
The season
In which your
Loved one died
Always brings
Them back to you . . .

The falling leaves
And crisp
Night air
Recall those moments
You drew closer
Embracing

The snow flakes
Whirling by your
Windows recall
The evenings
Of warm soup
And pleasant conversations

The birth of flowers
A beautiful bouquet
Recall your
Wedding or your
Garden or your
Loved ones favorite scent

The sweet grass
Of summer and
Fireflies in the dark
Bring them back . . .
If only for those
Short seasons . . . of yesterdays

⤳ *Wishes*

I wish I had known
How to live
Years wasted
A cemetery
With no one around
To mourn

I wish I had looked
At the world
About me
Seasons of change
Yet I
Remained frozen

I wish I had grieved
Until I was
Empty
Instead I held fast
To the past
And my funeral

Until one day
I awoke
The sun was still shining
Hope peeked
Through my curtains
Of darkness

My wish had been answered
For each time
I smile
You are my joy
My hopes
My dreams

ꙮ *Yesterday's Tomorrow*

Tomorrow came
But you did not return
How does one live
Without someone you love?
So empty—a grave
Without a coffin

A month disappeared
I marked the day
With wistful tears
How does one go on
And pretend nothing's changed?
A cemetery

A year went by
An anniversary
I wish never existed
How does one move on
And begin life again?
An obituary

Yesterday returned
In photographs and memories
As if you had never left
Tomorrow
For you lived in my heart
All along!

❧ *Never Gone*

Did you ever notice
Some things, some people
Are never gone?

A piece of music
So beautiful, it plays forever
In your mind

A well written book
So meaningful, it lives forever
In your thoughts

A favorite flower
So fragrant, it lives forever
In your senses

A happy memory
So joyful, it lives forever
In your heart

Your loved one
So alive, living forever
In your soul

❧ *Until We Meet Again*

Don't be afraid
To live again
Now that I
Am gone
Store our memories
In your soul
And open your
Heart
To this world

Don't be hesitant
To laugh again
For when I heard
Your laughter
You lit a candle
In my soul
So share
Your gift
With others

Don't be shy
To love again
Forever we
Will love
Each other
But while
We're apart
You need the
Strength of love

Never be afraid
To walk alone
To live this life
As well as you
Can—to laugh
And love
And remember . . .
Until we meet
Again

ᕙ *A Parting Look*

Waiting
For the time
Of parting
To come
And leave behind the day

Like curtains
Parting to gaze
At the garden
And people
Below, rushing on with life

Like flower petals
Parting to gaze
At the sun
And moon
Above, moving with the tide

Like heaven's clouds
Parting to gaze
At the souls
Who will someday come
The waiting over

In remembrance

of

September 11, 2001

∿ *Scattered*

The story unfolded
On the news
Scattered images
Pain
Tears
Tragedy

How shall they
Say goodbye
Loved ones
Vanished
A cloud
Of ashes

To say goodbye
We need
To touch
See
Remember
A funeral

Instead . . . a dead
Building
Sacred pieces
People's dreams
Scattered
Flower petals

In slow motion
The flower opens
Revealing
The soul
Reaching
For the heavens

A cloud
Steals the sun
Flower petals
Caught
In the winds
Drifting . . .

To eternity

❦ *Home for the Holidays*

I hate the holidays
This year
I dread pretending
I am happy
When all I can feel
Is you

I remember you sitting
Just there
Under the tree
The Christmas lights
Reflected
In your eyes

I lean down and place
A gift
Next to you
I smell the shampoo
So soft
In your hair

Christmas carols
Play in the background
But all
I can hear
Is your warm
Loving voice

We drink cider
Taste cookies
Giggle like
Children
Anticipation teasing
Your lips

Snow is falling
Christmas is calling
But I am not here
This year
For I've gone home
For the holidays

∾ *You are there*

When tragedy strikes
A flash of lightning
Hundreds are dead
Time stops
And we
Are suspended . . .

In memories
A summer breeze
As we walked
Along the beach
And we
Were captured . . .

By love
Brilliant autumn leaves
Falling to the earth
Silence
And we
Were reluctant . . .

To let go
For winter comes
And only the snow
Is bright
For I
Am interred . . .

In grief
Yearning for spring
To be alive
To feel thunder
And rain
And you . . .

Are there

ꙮ *Fly Away Home*

I loved the way
You walked
You bounced
As if so happy
No matter how
You really felt

I loved the way
You laughed
The sound
Tickled everyone
Giving sunshine
During a storm

I loved the way
You listened
You always
Gave time
A precious gift
Of love

I loved the way
You cried
When we
Said goodbye
To fly away
'Till tomorrow

I'll never forget
Watching you
Walk away
Never realizing
It was to be
My last image

Of you

~ *How I Wish*

There is mist
In the trees
Tonight . . .

Dead silence
How is it
That yesterday

You were here
Your voice
Saying goodbye

"See you tonight!"
The words linger
Haunting me

How I wish
I had known
You wouldn't return

How I wish
I had said
"I love you forever!"

How I wish
I could
Turn back time

And savor
Every moment
You were here

There is mist
In the trees
Tonight

. . . wishing
On stars

0-595-26583-9